D1173790

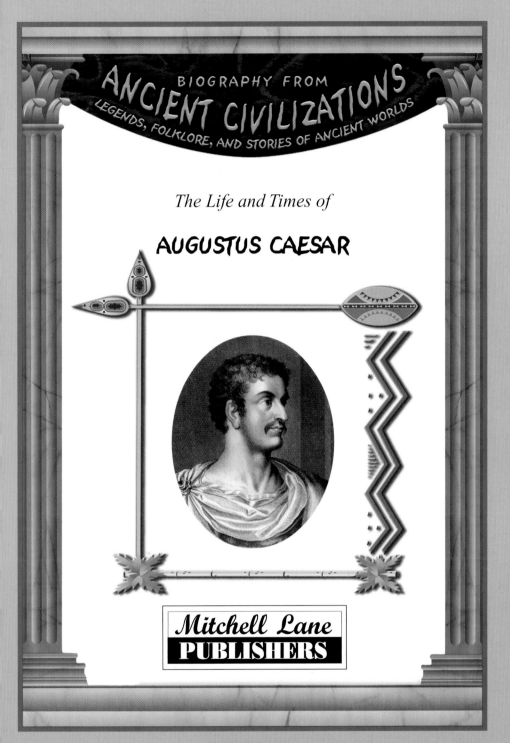

BIOGRAPHY FROM
ANCIENT CIVILIZATIONS
LEGENDS, FOLKLORE, AND STORIES OF ANCIENT WORLDS

The Life and Times of

AUGUSTUS CAESAR

Mitchell Lane
PUBLISHERS

P.O. Box 196
Hockessin, Delaware 19707

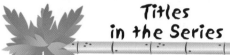

Titles in the Series

The Life and Times of:

BIOGRAPHY FROM
ANCIENT CIVILIZATIONS
LEGENDS, FOLKLORE, AND STORIES OF ANCIENT WORLDS

The Life and Times of

AUGUSTUS CAESAR

Jim Whiting

Mitchell Lane
PUBLISHERS

Printing   1   2   3   4   5   6   7   8

Library of Congress Cataloging-in-Publication Data

Whiting, Jim, 1943-
    The life and times of Augustus Caesar / Jim Whiting.
        p. cm. — (Biography from ancient civilizations)
    Includes bibliographical references and index.
    ISBN 1-58415-336-9 (library bound : alk. paper)
    1. Augustus, Emperor of Rome, 63 B.C. -14 A.D. —Juvenile literature. 2. Rome—History—Augustus, 30 B.C. -14 A.D.—Juvenile Literature 3. Emperors—Rome—Biography—Juvenile literature. I. Title. II. Series.
    DG279.W47 2005
    937'.07—dc22

                                              2004024593

ABOUT THE AUTHOR: Jim Whiting has been a journalist, writer, editor, and photographer for more than 20 years. In addition to a lengthy stint as publisher of *Northwest Runner* magazine, Mr. Whiting has contributed articles to the *Seattle Times*, *Conde Nast Traveler*, *Newsday*, and *Saturday Evening Post*. He has written and edited more than 130 Mitchell Lane titles. He lives in Washington state with his wife and two teenage sons.

PUBLISHER'S NOTE: This story is based on the author's extensive research, which he believes to be accurate. Documentation of such research is contained on page 47.

The internet sites referenced herein were active as of the publication date. Due to the fleeting nature of some web sites, we cannot guarantee they will all be active when you are reading this book.

BIOGRAPHY FROM ANCIENT CIVILIZATIONS
LEGENDS, FOLKLORE, AND STORIES OF ANCIENT WORLDS

The Life and Times of

AUGUSTUS CAESAR

*For Your Information

Julius Caesar survived an especially turbulent period in Roman history to become one of the city's most powerful leaders: too powerful, some of his opponents believed. They murdered him on the floor of the Roman Senate.

CHAPTER

THE KNIVES COME OUT

Like many eighteen-year-olds, Gaius Octavius was away from home, studying. Like many eighteen-year-olds, he had a job in addition to his studies. Like many eighteen-year-olds, he enjoyed leisure-time activities such as horseback riding, playing games, and socializing with his friends.

But there was one major difference between young Octavian, as he was more commonly known, and other eighteen-year-olds of his era. He was the grandnephew of Julius Caesar, one of the most powerful men in the world. On a day in March 44 B.C., he received the shocking news that his granduncle had been murdered.

Caesar's killers weren't fanatics or terrorists. They included some of Rome's most famous and respected men. They believed that they were protecting nearly five centuries of Roman history by slaying him.

The founding of Rome has traditionally been dated as 753 B.C. For more than two centuries afterward, the city was ruled by a succession of kings. Then in 509, the king was overthrown and Rome became a republic, governed by the Senate. To prevent anyone from assuming kinglike powers after that, every year the Senate appointed two of its members to serve as consuls, the city's highest officials. The Romans believed that having two consuls share power for just a single year would insure that neither one could obtain too much power.

When Rome and its surrounding territory were small, this system worked well. Then Roman armies began moving beyond the Italian peninsula and conquering ever-increasing amounts of land. Rome became much wealthier and more powerful. These conditions created chaos and turmoil in the government as rival factions competed for control. For decades before Julius Caesar's birth in 100 B.C., Roman politics had become more and more dangerous. Internal conflict and outright murder became commonplace. As a teenager, Julius Caesar wound up on a hit list put out by his political opponents. He managed to survive and began a steady rise in importance. In 48 B.C. he emerged victorious from a bloody civil war, then spent the next few years making himself even more powerful—too powerful, some senators believed. They believed that he wanted to take over the government of Rome and rule as an absolute dictator. They decided that the only way to eliminate the danger and maintain Rome as a republic was to assassinate him. After months of plotting, they carried out their attack. Julius Caesar was knifed to death as he presided over a meeting of the Senate.

At the time, Octavian was living in Apollonia, a city on the eastern coast of the Adriatic Sea. Julius Caesar had sent Octavian there to complete the studies he had begun while he was still a boy. More importantly, the young man had been placed in command of the Roman cavalry that was based there. The cavalry was part of a formidable army that Caesar planned to lead in a campaign against the Parthians, who had destroyed a Roman army in 53 B.C. at the battle of Carrhae in present-day Turkey. Only a handful of men survived to straggle back home, bearing news of one of the half-

Octavian was stationed at Apollonia during the time of his uncle's murder. After Octavian heard the news he quickly returned to Rome. By the time of Julius Caesar's death, the Roman Empire included nearly all the territory south of the Danube River and to the west of the Rhine River.

dozen worst military disasters in Rome's entire history. The Parthians had also captured the standards of the seven legions they had defeated. These standards had immense symbolic value, and Caesar wanted to reclaim them. He was about to leave Rome to begin the campaign when he was murdered.

The news of Caesar's death had been shocking enough to Octavian. There was an even greater shock. The teenager learned that Caesar had appointed him as his heir. He not only inherited a great deal of money, but he also became responsible for the family name of Caesar.

Octavian faced a dilemma. His mother and stepfather, well aware of the cutthroat nature of Roman politics, urged him not to become involved. They only wanted him to accept Caesar's wealth. It would provide him with enough money to live in comfort and security for the rest of his life. They pointed out that if Octavian accepted Caesar's family name, he would become responsible for avenging the assassination. They were afraid that against men two and three times his age, he would quickly be overcome and probably even killed.

Octavian didn't share their fears. In fact, he felt it was his duty to accept. As author John Carter points out, "Octavian's ambition had been stirred by Caesar's judgment of him and he asserted that it would be a crime, if Caesar had thought him fit to bear his name, to think otherwise himself."[1] There was probably another factor. Even if he had chosen not to become involved in politics, his new relationship with Caesar would have been obvious to Caesar's numerous enemies. They probably would have marked him for death no matter what he did. He chose to take on the enormous responsibility of being Caesar's heir.

He made an immediate return to Rome, even though crossing the Adriatic Sea at the end of winter was dangerous. The perils of a stormy sea crossing, however, paled in comparison to what he would face when he returned to Rome. He did have one immense asset: Caesar's name. Caesar had been very popular with many Romans, especially the soldiers. The troops gave Octavian a warm welcome every time he passed a group of them during his journey.

This popularity made him very valuable in the confusion that came after Caesar's assassination. Caesar's killers had been so concerned with getting rid of him that they hadn't thought much about what would happen afterward. They had left the city essentially without a leader.

Many Romans looked up to Mark Antony, a formidable politician who had been closely allied with Julius Caesar. After the assassination, Mark Antony delivered the funeral oration. Holding up the dead man's bloodstained clothing, he inflamed the crowd of Roman citizens who heard him. They became so angry that the conspirators had to flee Rome. Because of his prestige, Antony was able to bring some order out of the chaos that threatened to engulf the city. Soon he became very powerful.

For many senators, Mark Antony was becoming just as threatening as Caesar had been. One of Antony's opponents was Cicero, a senator who was considered the city's best public speaker. Cicero wasn't afraid to speak his mind, and some of the things he said about Antony were much worse than modern-day election insults. He welcomed the appearance of Octavian, believing the young man could be a useful tool. Octavian was quickly made a member of the Senate, even though he was far younger than the legal age. Cicero and other senators believed they could use the prestige of the Caesar name to gain enough support to oust Mark Antony. Then they could restore the republic. Once that had been done, Octavian's usefulness would be over. As Cicero said, the older men could "praise him, honor him, then get rid of him."[2]

Cicero was partly right. It was easy for him and other like-minded senators to praise and honor Octavian. But as events would demonstrate, it proved impossible to get rid of him. Octavian was a quick learner. He had to be in order to survive and thrive in the jungle of Roman politics.

"Those who scoffed at the sudden elevation of an untried boy to such an exalted position discovered to their peril that Octavian was an exceptionally hard, cunning, coldly ambitious young man, with a generous measure of cruelty in his character,"[3] writes historian William Klingaman.

Antony was among the ones who scoffed at Octavian. He had good reason. He resented Octavian because he felt that Julius Caesar should have preferred him to the boy. Antony had risked his life several times to support Caesar, both on the Senate floor and in battle. What had the boy ever done? he must have wondered.

Right away Octavian found himself in the midst of a lot of name-calling. Antony wasn't about to roll over and play dead in the face of the vicious personal attacks by Cicero and the other senators. He fought back, taking dead aim at the newcomer.

Mark Antony "slander[ed Octavian] with the claim that his great-grandfather had been a slave and that his father had been a money-changer specializing in the distribution of bribes before he broke into politics," writes historian Philip Matyszak. "As for his mother, alleged Antony, she was the daughter of a baker."[4] While such words may seem relatively harmless today, they were stinging rebukes among status-conscious Roman nobles.

The bitter conflict put Rome on the verge of yet another civil war. Mark Antony was forced to leave Rome, but he soon raised an army of supporters. With the two current consuls, Octavian led an army that pursued Mark Antony and defeated him in two battles. During these battles, both of the consuls were killed. Their deaths were somewhat suspicious. Some historians believe that Octavian arranged for their deaths so that the position of consul would be vacant. He had the ideal candidate: himself. Officially he was ineligible because he was far too young. That didn't stop him.

As ancient historian Suetonius writes, "[Octavian] created himself Consul, marched on Rome as though it was an enemy city, and sent messengers ahead in the name of his army to demand that the appointment should be confirmed. When the Senate hesitated to obey, one Cornelius, a centurion [an army officer] leading the deputation, opened his military cloak, displayed the hilt of his sword, and boldly said: 'If you do not make him Consul, this will!'"[5]

It was a remarkable accomplishment. In just over a year, Octavian had been transformed from an obscure teenager into one of the most powerful men in Rome.

But he still had a lot of work to do. By this time, Antony had forged an alliance with Lepidus, an important general and politician who had also been one of Caesar's strongest supporters. Octavian knew that the combined strength of the armies of these two men was more than his troops could handle. He quickly cut a deal with his opponents. The previous war of words was forgotten as Octavian, Mark Antony, and Lepidus formed what became known as the Second Triumvirate, which literally means "three men." In 60 B.C., Julius Caesar and two other important Romans, Pompey and Crassus, had formed the First Triumvirate. It became the dominant influence in Roman politics. The Second Triumvirate had the same purpose. Its three members held almost absolute power in Rome. They used their power to seek revenge on anyone against whom they held a grudge or to eliminate anyone who represented a threat to them.

In many cases, they abandoned men who had been their supporters—men such as Cicero, who was about to find out how ruthless Octavian really was. Shortly before the formation of the Second Triumvirate, Cicero wrote, "When we [the Senate] gave Octavian military command, we were in fact encouraging the hope with which his name [of Caesar] inspired us, and now that he has fulfilled these hopes, he has sanctioned the authority of our decree by his exploits." Cicero called him a "young man of great mind."[6]

Cicero was wrong in his judgment. Octavian's "great mind" was pointed in one direction: doing whatever would advance his own power. If the result was betraying people who thought of him as their friend, that didn't matter.

Not surprisingly, Antony wanted Cicero dead. That was fine with Octavian. Cicero was put to death. He was hardly alone. According to some estimates, more than 2,000 men—including 300 senators—were murdered. The triumvirs took their victims' lands and their wealth.

Octavian was probably motivated in this reign of terror by thoughts of his granduncle. After defeating his opponents during the civil war a few years earlier, Julius Caesar had executed some of them but allowed others to remain alive. Two of the men to whom Caesar had showed clemency—Brutus and Cassius—repaid his mercy by leading the conspirators and helping to stab him to death. Octavian had no intention of making the same mistake.

With their opponents in Rome crushed, the next step for the triumvirs was to go after Caesar's killers, who had assembled a formidable army under the leadership of Brutus and Cassius. The opposing forces met at the battle of Philippi in Greece in 42 B.C. According to some reports, Antony's army defeated Cassius's, while Brutus's forces won an initial victory over Octavian's troops. Antony came to the rescue and defeated Brutus. Rather than be captured, Cassius and Brutus committed suicide, and their armies surrendered.

It appeared that peace had finally returned to Rome.

It hadn't.

Rome's Legendary Founder

According to legend, Rome was founded in 753 B.C. by the twins Romulus and Remus. The two boys were the sons of the god Mars and a woman named Rhea Silvia. Her uncle, Amulius, was king of the Italian city of Alba Longa. He had overthrown Rhea Silvia's father Numitor and feared that the boys would grow up to overthrow him in turn. He put them in a small boat soon after they were born and set it adrift on the Tiber River, hoping it would overturn and the boys would drown.

Mars

The little boat drifted ashore, where a female wolf discovered the helpless infants. She "adopted" them and fed them with her milk. Later a shepherd found them and raised them. When they became young men, they killed Amulius and restored Numitor to his throne. Then they decided to establish their own city on the spot where the wolf had rescued them. As sometimes happens with brothers, they didn't get along. Remus made fun of the height of the walls that Romulus had started to build. Romulus was enraged and killed Remus.

Romulus finished building the new city and named it Rome, after himself. He encouraged exiles, criminals, and other desperate men to settle there. These men needed wives so that the population could increase. Romulus tricked a nearby tribe called the Sabines into coming to a feast. While the Sabine men were distracted, the Romans kidnapped their women and carried them back to the city. The Sabine leaders tried to get their women back and fought the Romans. By then the Sabine women had accepted their new husbands. They persuaded the men to stop fighting. Eventually the Sabines accepted Romulus as their king.

He proved to be an able leader. He is credited with developing the calendar the Romans used. After a long period of successful rule, he disappeared during a violent storm. The Romans revered him as a god named Quirinus.

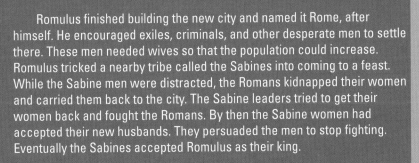

This picture of Augustus Caesar depicts him as a young man. Even then, he showed signs of the political greatness that would characterize his reign. He was the first of more than 60 Roman emperors and almost certainly the most outstanding.

CHAPTER
TWO

THE ROAD TO ACTIUM

Octavian was born on September 23, 63 B.C. In all likelihood, his birthplace was Rome. He came from a relatively obscure family. His grandfather had been a banker in a town outside of Rome and became wealthy through a number of successful land investments. But he had not been involved in politics. Octavian's father, whose full name was also Gaius Octavius, was different. He entered politics and became a member of the Senate. Octavian's mother was Atia. Her mother was Julia, Julius Caesar's sister. Octavian had two older sisters.

The elder Gaius Octavius appeared to be destined for great things in spite of the fact that he represented "new money" in a culture that placed a high value on tradition and inherited wealth. He took on a series of administrative positions of increasing importance. Many people expected him to be a consul someday. These expectations were cut short when he died in 59 B.C. His son was only four. Within two or three years, Atia married Marcus Philippus, who had been a consul himself.

Little is known of young Octavian's upbringing, though as the son and stepson of important noblemen he probably would have had a private tutor in such subjects as Greek, Latin, and public speaking. It didn't take him long to prove that he was an able student. When he was twelve, his grandmother Julia died. Octavian gave the funeral oration. That brought him to the attention of his granduncle, who began conferring military honors on him even though he was still too young to serve in the Roman army.

Soon after the funeral, Julius Caesar departed for Spain to fight yet another battle as he tried to consolidate his power. The daring boy followed him. As Suetonius explains, "Augustus followed with a very small escort, along roads held by the enemy, after a shipwreck, and in a state of semi-convalescence from a serious illness. This action delighted Caesar, who, moreover, soon formed a high estimate of Augustus' character apart from the energetic manner in which he had made the journey."[1]

As Caesar began preparing for his campaign against the Parthians, he sent Octavian ahead to Apollonia. There Octavian met two men who became very important in his later life: Agrippa and Maecenas. Naming Octavian head of the cavalry in spite of his limited experience shows how highly Caesar regarded the young man. As the events following Caesar's death dramatically demonstrated, this regard was well placed. Octavian quickly proved himself a worthy heir.

With their final opposition eliminated following the defeat of Brutus and Cassius, the Second Triumvirate held a meeting to divide up Rome's massive territories. As the senior member, Antony received the most profitable portion—Egypt, Greece, and other eastern lands. Lepidus was given North Africa, while Octavian took over Rome itself, the rest of Italy, and territories to the west such as Spain and Gaul (present-day France).

The loyalty of the three men to each other was soon tested as Octavian faced his first crisis of leadership. When the civil wars had begun several years earlier, Caesar promised land to the soldiers who supported him. Now it was up to Octavian to make good on the promise. There was enough land to go around. Unfortunately, it was already occupied by thousands of small farmers. They had to be evicted. Antony's wife Fulvia and his brother Lucius took advantage of the widespread dissatisfaction that this move created and led a revolt against Octavian. Historians are not sure if Antony himself was involved. Unlike his granduncle, Octavian wasn't an especially good military leader. Fortunately, he had someone who was. This was Agrippa.

The same age as Augustus, Agrippa was as gifted militarily as Octavian was politically. Under his leadership, the revolt was put down by the time Antony returned to Rome.

Fulvia had died during the revolt. To strengthen his bond with Octavian, Antony married Octavia, Octavian's sister. A little earlier, Octavian had married Claudia, Mark Antony's stepdaughter. He soon divorced her and married a woman named Scribonia. They had a daughter, Julia. Not long afterward, according to contemporary accounts, he grew tired of her nagging and divorced her, then found yet another wife. Her name was Livia Drusilla, and she was married to another man. She was only nineteen, but she already had a son—named Tiberius—and was pregnant with another son. It didn't matter to Octavian. While she had connections to a number of important families, there was more to the relationship than political considerations. Octavian apparently was genuinely in love with her. He insisted that she divorce her husband and marry him. It was a marriage that would endure for more than half a century.

In 37 B.C., Octavian, Antony, and Lepidus renewed their agreement for five more years. But beneath the surface, the triumvirate was about to fall apart. Soon after this agreement Antony sent Octavia back to Rome and began living openly with Cleopatra, the queen of Egypt, with whom he had been involved for several years. Cleopatra was no stranger to important Romans. A decade earlier, she had had an affair with Julius Caesar, which resulted in the birth of a son named Caesarion. As Egypt's ruler, Cleopatra also commanded great riches, which Antony needed for his plans. He realized that at some point he would have to go to war with Octavian, and the money would help him finance the large army he would require.

Octavian quickly took advantage of Antony's relationship with Cleopatra for propaganda purposes. He held up his sister as a wife who had been abandoned by a treacherous husband. He told the Romans that Antony's children with Cleopatra had already been appointed as rulers of part of the empire in the east even though they were still toddlers. Octavian even stole Antony's will from its supposedly secure resting place. According to its terms, Antony wanted to be buried in Egypt. There were rumors that Antony wanted to move the capital of the empire from Rome to Alexandria in Egypt, Cleopatra's home. All these factors, Octavian said, demonstrated that Antony was a dangerous man.

Antony did not make things any easier for himself on the battlefield. He wanted to increase his prestige by leading a campaign against the Parthians, trying to recover the standards the Romans had lost in 53 B.C. While his losses weren't as catastrophic as the ones in the earlier conflict, the Parthians forced him to retreat, and Antony suffered a loss of prestige.

With all of these factors in his favor, Octavian didn't have much trouble stirring up the people against Antony. Before turning his full attention to Antony, however, Octavian had other problems to deal with. Sextus Pompey—the son of Pompey, a member of the First Triumvirate who eventually became Julius Caesar's bitter rival— used his father's name and prestige to mount a challenge to

Octavian. This challenge was more difficult to overcome than the revolt led by Fulvia and Lucius had been. Once again, Agrippa's leadership was crucial as Octavian's forces finally defeated Sextus Pompey.

Now Octavian had to deal with Lepidus, who had always been the "junior partner" in the triumvirate. Lepidus had helped Octavian defeat Sextus Pompey. As a result, he found himself in command of a huge army. He felt he could finally stand up to Octavian.

Octavian may not have been a particularly good military man, but that didn't mean he wasn't brave. He went to Lepidus's camp and made a direct appeal to the soldiers, reminding them of their allegiance to Julius Caesar, his "father." It worked. Most of the men came over to his side. Lepidus soon realized that his situation was hopeless. He begged Octavian for his life. Somewhat uncharacteristically, Octavian agreed. He allowed Lepidus to live. At first he banished him, then he allowed him to return to Rome. Lepidus became *pontifex maximus*, the chief priest of the Roman religion, and held the position for the rest of his life.

Octavian knew that defeating Antony would be even more difficult. He spent several years building up a strong army and navy. Finally he was ready. Under the leadership of Agrippa, his forces met the combined forces of Antony and Cleopatra at Actium, a small port on the western coast of Greece, on September 2, 31 B.C.

When the outcome of the battle was still in doubt, Cleopatra's force of sixty ships unexpectedly burst through the middle of Octavian's fleet and headed for the open sea. Antony had to make an instant decision. He followed Cleopatra. With both of their leaders gone, their men had to surrender. Antony and Cleopatra fled to Egypt. Octavian knew he couldn't leave them there. With Egypt's immense wealth backing them, they could raise enough forces to challenge him again. Followed by a large army, he pursued them. Antony committed suicide rather than be taken prisoner. Cleopatra was captured. She knew that she would be taken to Rome and publicly humiliated. To avoid this fate, she had one of her servants carry a basket of figs past her guards. Coiled under the fruit was an asp, a highly poisonous snake. Cleopatra let it bite her and quickly died.

The victory brought tremendous wealth and prestige to Octavian and removed his last major opponent. To further secure his position, he ordered that Caesarion, the son of Julius Caesar and Cleopatra and therefore a potential rival, be strangled.

Rome had fought its final civil war. Decades of unrest had come to an end. In thirteen years, Octavian had achieved a level of power that few, if any, Romans had ever had. But he knew that he couldn't let down his guard. The example of his granduncle's death was a constant reminder of the dangers and uncertainties that accompanied such extreme power. There were still plenty of knives left in Rome.

Religion in Rome

Rome had many gods and goddesses. Most households had statues of private deities known as lares. The family would pray to these household guardians at a small shrine, asking them to keep them prosperous and protect them from evil.

There was also a public religion, with temples and elaborate ceremonies. As their power expanded, the Romans incorporated some of the religions of the people whom they conquered. The most important influence came from the Greeks. The Romans took over many Greek gods and goddesses and gave them different names. Zeus, the chief Greek god, became Jupiter. The name of his wife, Hera, was changed to Juno. She was especially important to women, safeguarding marriage and childbirth. Athena, the goddess of war, wisdom, and crafts, became Minerva.

Jupiter

Every year on January 1, a solemn procession made its way through the streets of Rome. When it reached the Capitoline Hill, several bulls were sacrificed to Jupiter. The hope was that Rome would be protected during the course of the upcoming year. These ceremonies were presided over by the *pontifex maximus,* the chief priest. The position was often filled by important political figures. Julius Caesar was one. Lepidus was another. So was Augustus Caesar.

In A.D. 392, the emperor Theodosius I declared Christianity as the official religion of Rome. In modern times, the Vatican City in Rome is the heart of Roman Catholicism. The Pope is often referred to as the pontiff, a title that comes from *pontifex maximus*.

The names of a number of Roman gods live on. The month of March is named for Mars, the god of war. Many people believe that June is named for Juno. Except for Earth, all of the planets in our solar system carry Roman names: Mercury (the messenger god and protector of travelers), Venus (the goddess of love), Mars, Jupiter, Saturn (god of the harvest), Uranus (the sky god), Neptune (god of the sea), and far-off Pluto (god of the underworld).

This statue of Augustus Caesar was created when he was at the peak of his power. He used this power to establish a period of peace and stability that lasted for several centuries. He also encouraged the growth of the arts. Many writers produced enduring poems and plays.

CHAPTER
THREE

FIRST AMONG EQUALS

The death of his most formidable rival put Octavian at the head of the Roman government. But he had to proceed cautiously. If he was as obvious in seeking power as Julius Caesar had been, the same fate could befall him. He openly proclaimed his allegiance to the forms of the republican government. For eight years, he appeared to be content with being named as consul. He even insisted on being called *princeps*, or "first citizen." Behind the scenes he maneuvered carefully to keep the real power in his own hands.

His first step after the deaths of Antony and Cleopatra was to make Egypt into a Roman province. Huge amounts of grain—assuring a steady food supply for Roman citizens—and vast sums of money were under his control. Then he set up a series of triumphs. These were mammoth parades and periods of thanksgiving for Roman victories.

For Roman citizens, there was plenty of cause for thanksgiving. For more than a century, the bitter divisions in Roman politics and the civil wars had cost countless lives. The unsettled conditions also affected people in their everyday lives. Now that Octavian had finally created peaceful conditions, Roman citizens seemed in the

Cleopatra is one of the most famous female rulers in history. She became queen of Egypt when she was only 17. She had love affairs with Julius Caesar and Mark Antony before her death at the age of 39.

mood to live under his rule—as long as he didn't appear to want to have complete power.

To increase his popularity, Octavian began a huge public works program. A nearby quarry at the town of Carrara provided an almost unlimited supply of excellent white marble. A number of spectacular public buildings began to emerge, paid for out of public funds. He also encouraged wealthy aristocrats to add their money to the building boom. Much later in life, he would say, "I found Rome built of bricks; I leave her clothed in marble."[1]

Despite all the lavish building projects that Octavian originated, his personal life was relatively simple. He lived in a modest home, rather than an elaborate palace. It wasn't entirely for image. According to Suetonius, "He was frugal and, as a rule, preferred the food of the common people, especially the coarser sort of bread, whitebait, fresh hand-pressed cheese, and green figs of the second crop; and would not wait for dinner, if he felt hungry, but would eat anywhere."[2] His one concession to vanity was wearing thick soles on his footwear so that he would appear taller than he actually was.

Even though the new buildings began to alter the Roman cityscape and the lives of the people began to improve, Octavian knew that memories fade fast. He had to appear to give up some of his power. Early in 27 B.C., after his victory at Actium, he said that he was restoring the government to the Senate and to the people. Perhaps in gratitude, the Senate returned the favor by giving him a new name. Some of the senators wanted to call him Romulus, after the legendary founder of Rome. But a senator named Plancus had another idea. He urged adding the name of Augustus, which means "revered" or "honored," to the already existing family name of Caesar.

There was probably another reason for preferring Augustus. Romulus had been a king. Octavian knew that any connection between himself and a king could be dangerous. Even so, he allowed himself to be called *imperator*, which means "supreme commander" and was reserved for the commander of an army fighting away from Rome. Traditionally, a general had to give back the title when he returned to the city. In a break with tradition, Augustus Caesar—it was the name by which he would be known for the rest of his life and down through history—was allowed to keep this title. It is the source of our modern word *emperor*.

In spite of what he said, Augustus wasn't giving up any of his power. In reality, he was still consul. Another, more important, fact was that he had set up two types of provinces: senatorial provinces, where the Senate appointed the governors; and imperial provinces, which were under Augustus's direct control. Imperial provinces were farther away from Rome, and nearly all the legions were stationed there. These troops had all sworn an oath of allegiance to Augustus rather than to Rome. The distance from Rome also reduced the possibility that they could come together under the control of a powerful enemy and threaten his position.

Four years after making these sweeping "changes," Augustus gave up the position of consul. During the era of the Republic, consul had been the most coveted position in the government. It conferred enormous prestige on the holder. Now Augustus held no official governmental titles. He didn't need any.

He used his position and his power to create enormous public games, many more than even the most free-spending of his predecessors had presented. These included gladiator combats, athletic contests, wild beast shows, and even mock naval battles on an artificial lake that had been dug up near the Tiber River. Tens of thousands of Romans flocked to them. Augustus made sure that everyone knew who was responsible for the good times they were enjoying.

Even though he was now extremely popular, in the back of his mind he knew that he was still vulnerable. He reorganized the Praetorian Guards, originally a small group of bodyguards. He expanded them to an elite force of nearly 10,000 men; their primary purpose was to ensure his safety.

With his base increasingly secure, he spent more and more time trying to improve living conditions in Rome and in the provinces. To guarantee that families had enough to eat, he gave out free grain to the city's households. He instituted a system of watchmen, so it became much safer to walk the streets even in the middle of the night. He created fire brigades to insure that the city's tightly packed, flimsy wooden apartment buildings would not erupt in flames. He added a new aqueduct, which brought extra fresh water into the city every day. He made efforts to clean up the Tiber River and keep it from flooding every spring. No detail was too minor to demand his attention. He personally oversaw everything from providing decorations for roadside statues of gods to controlling rabbits that destroyed crops in one of the provinces.

He also passed laws that promoted moral behavior. Some of these laws offered financial rewards for people to get married and have children. Others discouraged divorce and provided penalties for people who were caught in certain types of love affairs.

He was equally active in foreign policy. Rome still carried bitter memories of the defeat by the Parthians. Antony's failure hadn't helped Rome's reputation. Augustus felt compelled to do something. He realized that mounting an invasion would be very expensive, draining money from his domestic reforms. And there was no guarantee of success. In the year 20 B.C., Augustus concluded a treaty with the Parthians. They agreed to return the captured standards. In return, he guaranteed to respect the current borders. It was a brilliant move. He had secured the eastern border of the empire without losing a single man, a victory that he felt was as great as if he had achieved it in battle. He ordered huge celebrations.

Not long before, he had begun a similar effort to secure the empire's northern border. When he had assumed power, fierce German tribes roamed unchecked not far from the Italian peninsula. His first step was to push the frontier farther north. The Danube River, which flows east through central Europe and empties into the Black Sea, was a logical border. So was the Rhine River, which flows west and then turns north to the North Sea. Under the command of Augustus's stepsons, Tiberius and Drusus, Roman legions slowly forced the Germans back, well beyond the Danube. They also secured the border along the Rhine.

Local tribes fought back fiercely, but Drusus led a campaign that pushed beyond the Rhine to the Elbe River. Before he could consolidate his control of this region, he died. Tiberius replaced him and continued the campaign. Augustus was confident of eventual success.

Augustus wanted to make sure that people knew who was responsible for the prosperity they all shared. He erected statues of himself, both in Rome and in the provinces. His image appeared in paintings and on coins.

This effort seemed to be just as successful as all his others. As the Greek writer Strabo, who lived during this time, pointed out, "The Romans and their allies have never enjoyed such peace and prosperity as that provided by Caesar Augustus from the point when he acquired absolute dominion."[3]

Housing in Rome

Augustus boasted that he made Rome into a city of marble. It was—in its public places. For most of the city's residents, life revolved around tiny apartments that were far removed from the impressive public structures.

Typical apartment buildings, known as *insulae,* consisted of timber frames with brick facades and were built around a courtyard. They were several stories high and packed tightly together. Shops usually took up the ground floor, with stairs leading to the apartments—many of which had just a single room for an entire family—on the other floors. Light came from one or two small windows, which were often shuttered in winter to keep out the chill winds. Small braziers, similar to modern charcoal grills, created heat but gave off smoke. Oil-burning lamps provided some illumination and added to the amount of smoke in the rooms. There was no running water. A family member would carry a large urn to the public wells, fill it, and bring it back home. Few *insulae* had sanitary facilities. People either used public latrines or kept smelly chamber pots inside their apartments. When these containers were full, they were frequently emptied onto the street below. Because of the often flimsy construction, many *insulae* collapsed, killing or injuring their inhabitants. Fire was a constant danger.

Marble Columns

Wealthy Romans lived in large houses. The entrance room was known as an atrium. It was open to the sky and usually had a pool in the middle. Public areas in the front of the house provided plenty of space to entertain guests. These areas had elaborate murals on the walls, marble floors, and other expensive decorations. The private family rooms such as bedrooms and the kitchen were located in the rear and tended to be much plainer.

Rich or poor, Romans had one thing in common: They liked growing things. Well-to-do residents grew gardens next to their houses. Many *insulae* residents had window boxes with a few flowers.

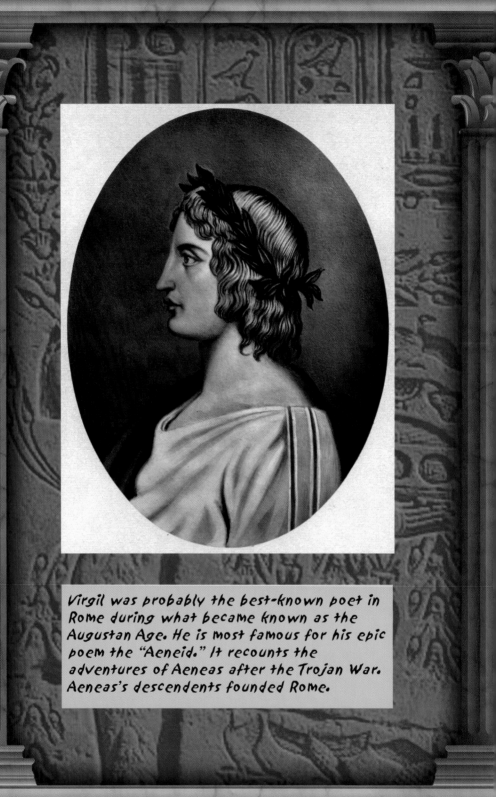

Virgil was probably the best-known poet in Rome during what became known as the Augustan Age. He is most famous for his epic poem the "Aeneid." It recounts the adventures of Aeneas after the Trojan War. Aeneas's descendents founded Rome.

CHAPTER
FOUR

THE AUGUSTAN AGE

Another way of promoting the image of Rome's greatness was through the arts. Led by Maecenas—another of Octavian's friends from his time in Apollonia—wealthy Romans were encouraged to spend large amounts of money to support talented writers. These writers often extolled their happiness in Rome's peace and prosperity and Augustus's role in bringing about these conditions. Another common theme was love poetry, in which the writers detailed their changing relationships with their "significant others."

Several of the best-known names in ancient literature date from this era, which became known as the Augustan Age. These included Horace, Tibullus, Propertius, and Ovid.

Probably the most famous was the poet Virgil. Born in 70 B.C., he had also lived through the civil wars and could appreciate the changes that Augustus had made. He wrote an epic poem called the *Aeneid*. Its central figure is Aeneas, a veteran of the Trojan War. After the city of Troy was destroyed by the Greeks, Aeneas had a number of adventures and finally wound up in Italy. Romulus and Remus, the city's legendary founders, were descended directly from him.

The poem thus linked Rome with ancient Greece, which was important culturally. It also gave the city a heroic past.

One of Augustus Caesar's most enduring legacies was established in 8 B.C. Soon after Julius Caesar was assassinated, a month was named for him. Augustus wanted the same honor.

Originally, the Roman calendar consisted of ten months. March was first, followed by April, May, and June. Then came Quintilis, Sextilis, Septembris, Octobris, Novembris, and Decembris. These six names came from the Latin words for "five" through "ten." These months kept their original names even after January and February were inserted before March to start the year, which was adjusted to include twelve months.

Shortly before his death, Julius Caesar reformed the calendar. Because the number of days in each year had varied, he standardized the length of a year to 365 1/4 days. He also decided that the odd-numbered months would have 31 days, while the even-numbered months would have 30. The one exception was February, which would have 29 days, 30 in leap years.

Quintilis had been renamed July to honor Julius Caesar. That made Sextilis, the month that followed July, the logical choice for Augustus's "month," since he had followed his granduncle. There was another reason. Sextilis was also the month in which Augustus had first been elected consul.

There was a glitch. July had 31 days, while Sextilis had 30. Augustus's ego would not allow "his" month to have one day less than his granduncle's. He took a day from February and added it to what became known as August.

That led to a further problem. July, August, and September would all have 31 days. Augustus did not want three successive months to be that long. He ordered that September would give up a day to October, and November would do the same to December. That is the arrangement we still use.

Despite all of his successes, Augustus had at least one failure. Like Julius Caesar, he didn't have a son to be his heir. In all their years of happy marriage, he and Livia had just one child, who had died soon after birth. That left Julia—his daughter from his second marriage—as his only living child. One of his sisters had a teenage son named Marcellus, so Augustus declared him as his heir. He ordered Marcellus to marry his daughter Julia. But Marcellus died within two years. Augustus then had Julia marry his friend Agrippa. They had two sons, Gaius and Lucius, and Augustus soon adopted them. That seemed to set the line of succession. In celebration, he built a large monument called the *Ara Pacis* (Altar of Peace). It depicted Augustus and the members of his family. Augustus and Livia represented the strength of the present era. The children showed that this strength would continue long into the future.

A few years later, his plan began to unravel. Agrippa died in 12 B.C. Augustus forced Livia's son Tiberius to divorce a wife he loved and marry Julia. Tiberius also became the guardian of Gaius and Lucius. Tiberius soon rebelled and went into voluntary exile on the island of Rhodes. That was bad enough. Even worse was Julia's behavior. After three forced marriages, she was fed up. She began a series of notorious love affairs that embarrassed her father, especially since he was trying to set an example of morality. Soon Augustus was fed up. He banished her to an island, where guards kept her away from men.

She wasn't the only source of embarrassment. Julia had a daughter, also named Julia, who began embarrassing Augustus with behavior all too similar to her mother's. He sent her into exile too.

At least the line of succession still appeared to be secure, with Gaius and Lucius growing into manhood. It seemed appropriate that Augustus acquired yet another title in 2 B.C.: *Pater Patriae* (Father of the Fatherland). But the "father" was now in his mid-sixties and showing his age. As writer William Klingaman says, "The ruler of the Roman empire seemed to live his nights and days in a constant state of nervous tension, suffering from recurrent bouts of wakefulness, kidney stones, and a sort of chronic asthma that struck him every spring. He was almost blind in his left eye and had lost nearly all of his teeth, and those that remained were yellow and rotting. But Augustus was still alive and the republic and his enemies were dead."[1]

Unfortunately, his heirs would also soon be dead.

Ovid and the Metamorphoses

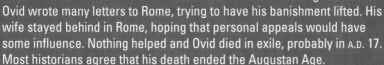

Born in 43 B.C., the same year that Augustus began his rise to power, Ovid was fortunate to grow up in a peaceful era. As the son of a nobleman, he was originally destined for a career in politics, but he abandoned his studies to become a poet. He traveled widely as a young man and soon made his mark through his love poetry. His best-known early work was the *Amores* (Loves), which was published when he was twenty-four. With the deaths of Virgil (19 B.C.) and Horace (8 B.C.), Ovid became the city's most prominent poet.

Ovid

Not everyone was happy with what he wrote. He had a talent for vivid and explicit descriptions. Some of his works shocked conservative Romans. He eventually angered Augustus, who banished him to a remote location on the western shore of the Black Sea in A.D. 8. No one knows what the actual reason was, though it is likely that his poems were too "X-rated" for Augustus's taste. Ovid wrote many letters to Rome, trying to have his banishment lifted. His wife stayed behind in Rome, hoping that personal appeals would have some influence. Nothing helped and Ovid died in exile, probably in A.D. 17. Most historians agree that his death ended the Augustan Age.

His most famous work is the *Metamorphoses.* This long narrative poem begins with the creation of the world and ends with the reign of Augustus. Many of the subjects are legendary or mythological. The title comes from a Greek word that means "to change shape," and many of the characters in the stories undergo extreme physical change, such as a nymph who is changed into a tree. The poem concludes with the words, "My name and fame are sure: I shall have life."[2]

These words proved to be prophetic. Ovid was especially popular during the Middle Ages, and many people still enjoy reading his work. He has also inspired a number of other poets.

This is a portrait of Tiberius, who succeeded Augustus Caesar. He was the son of Livia, Augustus's wife. Tiberius had a reputation as an excellent military commander and led a number of successful campaigns before becoming emperor in 14 A.D.

CHAPTER
FIVE

TIBERIUS AND TRAGEDY

Lucius died in A.D. 2, and Gaius died two years later. Augustus's stock of potential heirs was almost exhausted. A few weeks after learning of Gaius's death, Augustus legally adopted Tiberius—who had returned to Rome after Lucius died—as his son. Soon afterward, he sent him on an important mission.

By this time, Augustus's main concern was with the empire's northern border. More than a decade earlier, Tiberius and his brother Drusus had pushed beyond the Danube and the Rhine into the German wilderness. While the area remained relatively quiet for several years, nearly a third of the Roman army was stationed there.

There was good reason. Some of the tribes were conducting raids across the Rhine River into Gaul, the province that Julius Caesar had subdued more than half a century earlier. Augustus wanted to end those raids. More importantly, he wanted to add Germany to the list of Roman provinces. With Germany secure, Rome could expand even farther, into present-day Poland. Augustus sent Tiberius to Germany to carry out these missions.

At first, all went well. Tiberius was an excellent and well-respected general. His legions won a succession of battles. Within two years, the Romans were about to attack the final remaining major tribe when Tiberius was suddenly called away. A revolt in some newly acquired territories farther south threatened Rome itself. Augustus desperately needed Tiberius to return and defend the city. In three years of hard fighting, Tiberius overcame the resistance. He returned to Rome in triumph in the summer of A.D. 9.

Within a few days, the civic celebrations were interrupted by the arrival of horrible news. Three full legions—more than 15,000 men—under the command of Quintilius Varus had been slaughtered in Germany's Teutoburg Forest. It was a catastrophic defeat. Rome panicked. The entire Italian peninsula appeared to lie open to invasion.

The news had a profound personal effect on Augustus. According to Suetonius, "It is said that he took the disaster so deeply to heart that he left his hair and beard untrimmed for months; he would often beat his head on a door, shouting: 'Quintilius Varus, give me back my legions!' and always kept the anniversary as a day of deep mourning."[1]

Of course, there was no way that Augustus could get his legions back. At this point in his life, there was another thing he couldn't get back either: his health. Augustus became too weak to go to the Senate. His home became the center of the empire. Then in early August in the year 14, he felt well enough to accompany Tiberius on a trip.

The reprieve was an illusion. He became far too ill to travel back to Rome. One of his estates was nearby. He was carried there and put to bed in the same room where his father had died many years earlier. He urgently recalled Tiberius and spent some time with his heir, offering last-minute advice. Then he summoned a group of friends. According to Suetonius, he asked them, "Have I played my part in the farce of life creditably enough?" Moments later he added the typical final line of Roman plays: "If I have pleased you, kindly signify/Appreciation with a warm goodbye."[2]

His last words were to his wife: "Goodbye, Livia: never forget our marriage."[3] Moments later, he was dead. The month in which he had enjoyed his first great triumphs was also the month in which he died. In fact, some members of the Senate wanted to transfer the name August to September. That way the month named for Augustus would honor his birth, rather than his death. It didn't happen.

Historian Michael Grant sums up the effects of Augustus Caesar's life. "By his reorganization of the entire machinery of civilian government, he had proved himself one of the most gifted administrators the world has ever seen and the most influential single figure in the entire history of Rome. The gigantic work of reform that he carried out in every branch of Italian and provincial life not only transformed the decaying republic into a regime with many centuries of life ahead of it, but also created a durable efficient Roman peace."[4]

This peace, which became known to history as the *Pax Romana*, provided several hundred years of harmony inside Rome's borders. It stands as one of history's most notable accomplishments.

As author Phil Grabsky notes, "Without Augustus, the death of Julius Caesar could perhaps have caused the Empire to fragment into a host of small states and warring kingdoms. But his force of personality, and his brilliance as an administrator, governor, manipulator, had not only held the Empire together but so strengthened it that it would last for another five centuries in the West and even longer in the East."[5]

More than sixty emperors ruled Rome after Augustus's death. Not a single one of them left behind such an enduring legacy.

FYI
For Your Info

The Disaster in Teutoburg Forest

In seeking to extend the empire's border to the Elbe River, Augustus made a serious miscalculation. He selected Quintilius Varus to replace Tiberius as the commander of Roman forces in Germany. Varus, whose influence probably came from marrying Augustus's grandniece, was an administrator with little experience leading troops in the field.

In turn, Varus made some serious miscalculations. He underestimated both the fighting strength of the German tribes and the depth of their hatred for the Romans. Even worse, he depended on bad intelligence. A German leader named Arminius, who had supported Rome and had even been granted Roman citizenship, told him that some nearby tribes were in rebellion and needed to be suppressed. Arminius added that it would be an easy job for Varus's three battle-hardened legions, which totaled more than 15,000 experienced soldiers.

The Elbe River

Another German warned Varus that Arminius was lying. Varus laughed him off. Refusing to take elementary military precautions such as sending out scouts, Varus confidently plunged into the thick Teutoburg Forest. The trail was narrow and Varus's men were stretched out over several miles. In a violent thunderstorm, torrential rains turned the ground to mush. The Romans and their wagons could barely move.

Suddenly thousands of screaming German warriors poured arrows and spears into the Roman troops. Arminius had led Varus into an ambush. Because they were so spread out, it was almost impossible for the Romans to fight back. Other German tribes quickly heard of the legions' predicament. This was their chance to take revenge. As the slaughter went on, Varus committed suicide. A few Romans surrendered. They were beheaded, hanged, or crucified. A handful of women and children managed to flee and brought word of the disaster.

The defeat had a profound effect on European and world history. Germany developed without the influence of Rome. Its language, culture, and beliefs were very different from those of countries such as France and Spain, which had been part of the Roman Empire. These differences would culminate in the twentieth century when Germany twice invaded France during World War I and World War II, the two most destructive conflicts in human history.

Chronology

B.C.

63	Born on September 23 in Rome as Gaius Octavius
48	Puts on toga virilis, the Roman symbol of manhood, for the first time
45	Is named heir of Julius Caesar
44	After Caesar dies, inherits Caesar's name, wealth, and responsibilities
43	Elected as consul; forms Second Triumvirate with Lepidus and Mark Antony
42	Along with Mark Antony, defeats Julius Caesar's assassins Brutus and Cassius in the battle of Philippi
40	Marries Scribonia
39	Birth of daughter Julia
38	Marries Livia Drusilla
36	Defeats Sextus Pompey and, separately, Lepidus
31	Defeats Mark Antony and Cleopatra at the battle of Actium
29	Annexes Egypt as a province of Rome
27	Renamed Augustus; becomes virtual emperor
23	Nephew Marcellus dies
20	Achieves diplomatic settlement with Parthia, which secures Rome's eastern boundary
18	Introduces moral legislation
17	Adopts grandsons Gaius and Lucius as heirs
12	Becomes pontifex maximus after the death of Lepidus
11	Forces Julia and Tiberius to marry
9	Stepson Drusus dies
2	Confers title Pater Patriae on himself; exiles daughter Julia

A.D.

2	Death of Lucius
4	Death of Gaius; names Tiberius as his heir
8	Exiles Ovid
9	Grieves over loss of three legions at Teutoburg Forest

Timeline in History

B.C.	
106	Cicero, a famous Roman orator and politician, is born.
100	Julius Caesar is born.
83	Mark Antony is born.
73	Spartacus leads an uprising of his fellow slaves; he wins several victories but is captured and put to death two years later.
70	Roman poet Virgil is born.
69	Eygptian queen Cleopatra is born.
63	Syria becomes a Roman province.
60	Julius Caesar, Crassus, and Pompey form the First Triumvirate.
58	Julius Caesar begins his conquest of Gaul (present-day France); it ends six years later and establishes his power.
49	Julius Caesar crosses the Rubicon River to begin civil war with Pompey.
44	Julius Caesar is assassinated by a group of Roman senators who fear that he has become too powerful.
43	Roman poet Ovid is born.
40	Mark Antony marries Octavia, Octavian's sister; he later deserts her and marries Cleopatra.
19	Virgil dies.
4	Roman statesman and playwright Seneca the Younger is born.
A.D.	
14	Tiberius becomes emperor.
16	Roman poet Marcus Manilius names diamonds, using the Latin word adamas, which means "hardest metal."
17	Ovid dies.
37	Tiberius dies and Caligula, his nephew, becomes emperor.
41	Caligula is assassinated; Claudius I becomes emperor.

Timeline in History

46	Greek biographer Plutarch is born.
43	Romans begin full-scale invasion of Britain and found the city of Londinium (present-day London).
54	Nero, a distant relative of Augustus Caesar, becomes the Roman emperor.
64	A fire destroys much of Rome; Nero blames Christians for the blaze and begins to persecute them.
68	Nero commits suicide.

Glossary

centurion	(sen-CHUR-ee-un)—the commander of a century, the basic unit of the Roman army, which consisted of 80 to 100 men.
clemency	(CLEH-mun-see)—an act of mercy.
consuls	(KAHN-suls)—two members of the Roman Senate, each appointed to a one-year term, who exercised primary administrative control over the government.
legions	(LEE-juns)—the primary divisions of the Roman army, each containing about 5,000 men.
oration	(o-RAY-shun)—a formal, very dignified public speech.
propaganda	(prah-puh-GAN-duh)—biased statements that are intended to influence the way that people think; they often either distort the truth or contain outright lies.
standards	(STAN-durds)—emblems, usually mounted on poles, that represent military units; they are often used as rallying points and contain immense symbolic value.

Chapter Notes

CHAPTER ONE   THE KNIVES COME OUT

1. John M. Carter, *The Battle of Actium* (London: Hamish Hamilton, 1970), p. 32.

2. Phil Grabsky, *I, Caesar: Ruling the Roman Empire* (London: BBC Books, 1997), p. 62.

3. William Klingaman, *The First Century* (New York: HarperCollins, 1990), p. 20.

4. Philip Matyszak, *Chronicle of the Roman Republic* (London: Thames & Hudson, 2003), p. 227.

5. Suetonius, *The Twelve Caesars,* translated by Robert Graves (New York: Penguin Books, 1957), p. 67.

6. Matyszak, p. 229.

CHAPTER TWO   THE ROAD TO ACTIUM

1. Suetonius, *The Twelve Caesars,* translated by Robert Graves (New York: Penguin Books, 1957), p. 57.

CHAPTER THREE   FIRST AMONG EQUALS

1. Suetonius, *The Twelve Caesars,* translated by Robert Graves (New York: Penguin Books, 1957), p. 69.

2. Ibid., pp. 96–97.

3. Phil Grabsky, *I, Caesar: Ruling the Roman Empire* (London: BBC Books, 1997), p. 83.

CHAPTER FOUR   THE AUGUSTAN AGE

1. William Klingaman, *The First Century* (New York: HarperCollins, 1990), p. 17.

2. Ovid, *The Metamorphoses of Ovid,* translated by Allen Mandelbaum (New York: Harcourt Brace & Company, 1993), p. 549.

CHAPTER FIVE   TIBERIUS AND TRAGEDY

1. Suetonius, *The Twelve Caesars,* translated by Robert Graves (New York: Penguin Books, 1957), p. 65.

2. Ibid., p. 110.

3. Ibid.

4. Michael Grant, *History of Rome* (New York: Charles Scribner's Sons, 1978), p. 258.

5. Phil Grabsky, *I, Caesar: Ruling the Roman Empire* (London: BBC Books, 1997), pp. 96–97.

For Further Reading

For Young Readers

Greenblatt, Miriam. *Augustus and Imperial Rome.* Tarrytown, New York: Benchmark Books, 2000.

Hicks, Peter. *Gods and Goddesses in the Daily Life of the Ancient Romans.* Columbus, Ohio: Peter Bedrick Books, 2003.

James, Simon. *Ancient Rome.* New York: Viking, 1992.

Lively, Penelope. *In Search of a Homeland: The Story of the Aeneid.* New York: Delacorte Press, 2001.

Nardo, Don. *The Age of Augustus.* San Diego: Lucent Books, 1997.

Walworth, Nancy Zinsser. *Augustus Caesar.* Broomall, Pennsylvania: Chelsea House, 2002.

Works Consulted

Carter, John M. *The Battle of Actium.* London: Hamish Hamilton, 1970.

Grabsky, Phil. *I, Caesar: Ruling the Roman Empire.* London: BBC Books, 1997.

Grant, Michael. *History of Rome.* New York: Charles Scribner's Sons, 1978.

Hyslop, Stephen G., and Brian Pohanka. *Timeframe 400 B.C.–A.D. 200: Empires Ascendant.* Richmond, Virginia: Time-Life Books, 1987.

Klingaman, William K. *The First Century.* New York: HarperCollins, 1990.

Matyszak, Philip. *Chronicle of the Roman Republic.* London: Thames & Hudson, 2003.

Ovid. *The Metamorphoses of Ovid.* Translated by Allen Mandelbaum. New York: Harcourt Brace & Company, 1993.

Southern, Pat. *Augustus.* New York: Routledge, 1998.

Suetonius. *The Twelve Caesars.* Translated by Robert Graves. New York: Penguin Books, 1957.

On the Internet

The History Guide: *Lectures on Ancient and Medieval European History,* "Augustus Caesar and the *Pax Romana*"

http://www.historyguide.org/ancient/lecture12b.html

Octavian/Augustus

http://janusquirinus.org/Octavian/OctavianHome.html

PBS: *The Roman Empire*

http://www.pbs.org/empires/romans/empire/

Timeless Myths. *Classical Mythology,* "Tales of Rome"

http://www.timelessmyths.com/classical/rome.html

Index